# LAID-BACK SKIER

❄ *iii* ❄

# LAID-BACK SKIER

### By Colleen Smith

**Friday Jones**
**:: PUBLISHING ::**

Denver, Colorado, U.S.A.
FridayJonesPublishing.com

❄ *v* ❄

First printing 2011.
FridayJonesPublishing.com

Cover design by Colleen Smith and Nancy Benton
Cover images copyright © 2011 by Colleen Smith

Library of Congress Cataloging-in-Publication Data

Smith, Colleen
Laid-Back Skier/Colleen Smith
Denver, CO: Friday Jones Publishing, 2010.

p. cm.
ISBN-13: 978-0-9844289-3-9
ISBN: 0-9844289-3-3
Library of Congress Catalog Number: 2011931497

*For my ski buddies:*
*Dr. Joel Cooperman,*
*Elizabeth Logan Edwards, and*
*Clifford Edwards, an instructor with*
*Vail Snowsports School.*

# THE NATURE OF ALPINE SKIING: SKI TIPS AND TALES

By Colleen Smith

**A**lpine skiing provides sporting fun, and also a perfect metaphor for life: I choose my line; I decide details as I turn my way down a mountainside; I must respond—and quickly—to a lot of obstacles I didn't see coming.

Sometimes, I follow in another's tracks. Sometimes, I break my own trail. Occasionally, I tumble; but I pick myself up, dust the snow off, start again.

And as with anything else in life, practice makes progress. Years ago, I could not imagine warming up on black diamond runs, but now I do just that. And once I've lived to tell the tale of picking my way down through deep powder or Volkswagen Beetle-sized bumps, everything else seems like a catwalk.

Much like life.

For me, downhill skiing is uplifting and downright inspiring. I can't get enough of the exhilarating sensation of gliding through glades, schussing past rock formations, strafing the winter wonderland.

Skiing's visual rewards include privileged vistas of jagged mountain ranges, spruce saddles, and vast valleys only observable from on top of the world. Sometimes, I watch cloudscapes. Sometimes, if the sky went any bluer, it would be purple. Ravens wheel overhead in the rarefied air. The occasional red fox dashes over a snowdrift into the woods. (I keep

looking for a lynx.)

The gondola sails through the treetops of dense pine and aspen forests with the occasional bead tree. Even the lift lines entertain with colorful ski togs and equipment, now more creatively designed than ever.

Maybe, as one New Age friend insists, the feel-good nature of skiing owes to all those crystals. A snowflake, naturally, is a crystal.

To ski is to enter another reality.

The alpine skiing reality excludes many. The physical demands of alpine skiing are considerable. The sport obviously demands a certain degree of athleticism. Just walking up and down stairs in clumsy ski boots while shouldering weighty skis and wielding awkward poles can prove daunting. Though I'm 50, while skiing, I feel like a kid. Afterwards? A senior citizen. Hot tubs and epsom salts help.

Downhill skiing also makes psychological demands. To ski, one must face fear, yet not focus on the fearful. Stepping into a mountainside's gravity field requires confidence and builds confidence.

The ski was invented before the wheel; and skiing originally was more about survival than sport. When skiing shifted from a utilitarian endeavor to recreation, the human spirit spurred skiers to go faster, into the steep and the deep, off jumps, and through impossibly tight slalom turns à la Olympians.

But even basic alpine skiing requires focus. Downhilling requires me to remain present in each moment, considering every turn rather than the never-ending-to-do-list normally looping in my head. When I ski, each turn helps wipe clean the cluttered slate of my mind because I'm concentrating, instead, on my skiing. Instant by instant, I'm taking in the terrain, finding balance in space, and maneuvering to avoid life-threatening obstacles. While I'm working up a ski sweat, it's almost impossible to sweat deadlines or other day-to-day details.

As any alpine skier knows, positive thinking is powerful. One must focus on the fall line, but not on falling. Yet, if one skis, one falls. Sooner or later, one crosses tips, catches an edge, or executes a face-plant. It's not a matter of if, but when. Alpine skiers risk almost as many possible injuries as there are pinecones in the forest. They accept inherent danger because of the pay-off: Finding one's rhythm in the snow on the slopes can feel like flying. Or waltzing with the mountain.

Many traditions associate mountaintops with divinity. For me, skiing imparts a spiritual sense of freedom.

Of course, alpine skiing is not free. I've never participated in a sport that requires so much gear. And the equipment is not inexpensive. Nor are lift tickets, parking fees, or lunch in the ski lodge.

But the alpine skiing experience is priceless, which is why—despite costs plus hassles plus risks plus severe winter weather conditions—so many people return time and time again to the

slopes. You can't put a dollar amount on the liberating sensation and inspiration found only in downhill skiing.

The mountain will always be new, always presenting unpredictable challenges. Skiing humbles me, but no other sport has ever given me such a sense of accomplishment. After a day on the slopes, the celebratory après ski scene caps the peak experience with the camaraderie of rosy-cheeked, adrenaline-charged alpine people comparing ski tips and tales in hot tubs or over hot toddies.

Typically, after several consecutive days of skiing, on my way back down from the mountains, my spirits sink low. My inner Austrian envies ski bums. I resent the flat landscape, the smog, this other reality and its responsibilities.

But I also understand that as in skiing, so in life: It's all about balance. As in skiing, so in life: Know when to stop. *Wag your ski tales.*

— **Colleen Smith**
Denver, Colorado, USA
February 2011

This essay appeared in a slightly different form in *The Denver Post* in December 2010 under the headline *"Skiing: An elevated state."*

*As in skiing, so in life:*
GET THE BIG PICTURE.

As in skiing, so in life:
KNOW THE RULES.

_As in skiing, so in life:_

BE CONFIDENT.

*As in skiing, so in life:*

BE PREPARED.

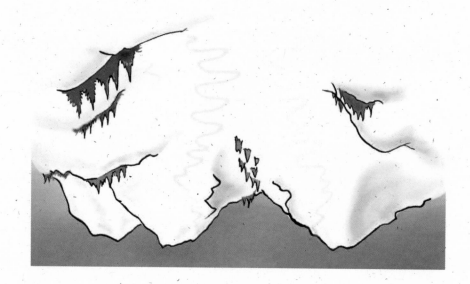

*As in skiing, so in life:*
MAKE SOME TRACKS.

As in skiing, so in life:
STAY HYDRATED.

*As in skiing, so in life:*
KN⦾W H⦾W T⦾ ST⦾P.

*As in skiing, so in life:*
THE BOTTOM PROVIDES A CHANCE TO GO TO THE TOP AGAIN.

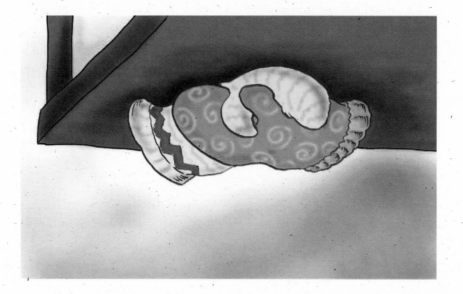

*As in skiing, so in life:*
SHARING THE EXPERIENCE
DOUBLES THE JOY.

As in skiing, so in life:
RELAX INTO
YOUR STANCE.

As in skiing, so in life:
KEEP YOUR BALANCE.

*As in skiing, so in life:*
ACKNOWLEDGE THOSE
WHO HELP YOU.

As in skiing, so in life: RESPECT OTHERS.

*As in skiing, so in life:*

TAKE CALCULATED RISKS.

*As in skiing, so in life:*
APPRECIATE THE SCENERY.

*As in skiing, so in life:*

KEEP TURNING.

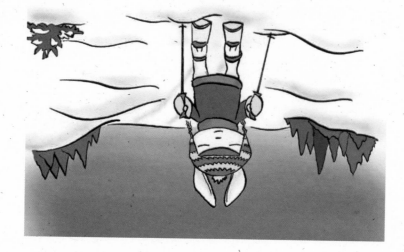

As in skiing, so in life:
GET CENTERED.

*As in skiing, so in life:*

KNOW YOUR LIMITS.

As in skiing, so in life:
KNOW THE TERRAIN.

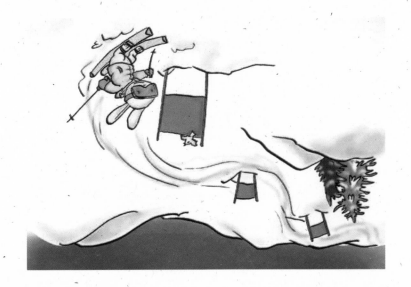

*As in skiing, so in life:*
DIFFICULT RUNS
MAKE EVERYTHING ELSE
SEEM EASIER.

As in skiing, so in life:
PUSH YOURSELF.

As in skiing, so in life:
REMAIN IN CONTROL.

As in skiing, so in life:
PRACTICE MAKES
PROGRESS.

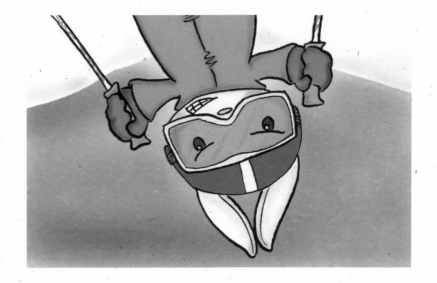

As in skiing, so in life:

STAY FOCUSED.

As in skiing, so in life:
DON'T HOLD YOUR BREATH;
ALLOW YOUR BREATH TO BE
TAKEN AWAY.

*As in skiing, so in life:*
ENJOY EXHILARATION.

As in skiing, so in life:
THE SNOWBALL EFFECT
IS REAL.

As in skiing, so in life:
TAKE A BREAK.

*As in skiing, so in life:*

LEAD WITH YOUR HEART.

As in skiing, so in life:
CHALLENGE YOURSELF.

As in skiing, so in life:
FACE YOUR FEARS.

*As in skiing, so in life:*

TAKE A LESSON.

*As in skiing, so in life:*
KEEP YOUR HEAD UP.

*As in skiing, so in life:*
PICK A PATH.

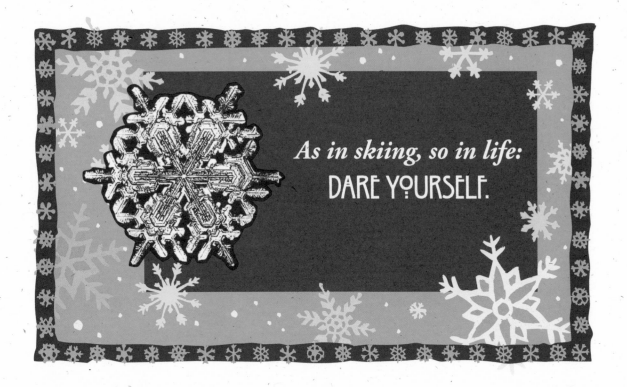

As in skiing, so in life:
DARE YOURSELF.

As in skiing, so in life:
WHEN YOU FALL,
GET UP AGAIN.

*As in skiing, so in life:*
SMILE AND ENJOY
THE RIDE.

# Skiers' Checklist: Essentials, Incidentals and Extras

**Essentials:**
- ☐ Skis
- ☐ Board
- ☐ Boots
- ☐ Poles
- ☐ Pass
- ☐ Helmet
- ☐ Goggles/Sunglasses
- ☐ Mittens or gloves
- ☐ Waterproof top layer
- ☐ Ski socks
- ☐ Lip balm
- ☐ Sunscreen
- ☐ Cash or credit card
- ☐ Cell phone

**Incidentals:**
- ☐ Glove liners
- ☐ Hand-warmers
- ☐ Toe-warmers
- ☐ Neck gaiter
- ☐ Balaclava
- ☐ Mid-layer
- ☐ Base layer
- ☐ Water bottle or CamelBak®
- ☐ Microfiber lens-cleaning cloth
- ☐ Tissues
- ☐ Bandana
- ☐ Camera

**Extras:**
- ☐ Boot carriers
- ☐ Whistle
- ☐ Avalanche beacons
- ☐ Powder cables
- ☐ Chewing gum or throat lozenges
- ☐ Snacks
- ☐ Energy bars, powdered drink mix or other nutritional supplement
- ☐ Ski cinches
- ☐ Tea bag, hot chocolate mix
- ☐ Soup envelope for frugal lunch

## SKI JOURNAL

# SKI JOURNAL

SKI JOURNAL

## ABOUT THE AUTHOR, ART DIRECTOR, PUBLISHER

COLLEEN SMITH, an award-winning author and art-director, earned her B.A. in English and studied fiction and poetry at the renowned Iowa Writer's Workshop. *Glass Halo*, Smith's critically acclaimed first novel, was named a finalist for the 2010 Santa Fe Writers Project Literary Award. The author lives in a Denver, Colorado, historic district and is an avid alpine skier, gardener, traveler, and yogini. She founded Friday Jones Publishing and contributes regularly to many publications, specializing in articles about arts and entertainment, gardening and fitness. Smith serves on the board of Metro Infanta Foundation for the Philippines and does pro bono work for Colorado Vincentian Volunteers.

Photo by James Baca

# About the Illustrator

Hailing from the Deep South, PATTY LEIDY, a nationally published cartoonist, now calls Denver her home. Preferring to work "old school," Patty and her ink-stained fingers can be found haunting local coffee houses in search for the perfect over-heard conversation quote for her latest comic strip. She thinks rabbits are the cutest things ever and though having never skied a day in her life, thinks snow bunnies on the slopes are naturals. This is her first book project with The Friday Jones Players.

# ABOUT THE DESIGNER

NANCY BENTON, a graphic designer, has collaborated with Colleen Smith for 21 years. Originally from Michigan, she graduated from Western Michigan University in 1981, with a BFA in Graphic Design. Nancy lives and works from her home in Parker, Colorado. She enjoys alpine skiing, as well as Nordic skiing and snowshoeing. She said, "Skiing is a wonderful way to explore the snowy mountains and enjoy winter beauty in the Colorado high country."

# Author's Acknowledgments

Profound gratitude goes out to the Friday Jones Players—Jesse Krieger, Andrea Collatz, Morgan Huston, and Roseanna Frechette—Tale-waggers extraordinaire.

Thank you to Nancy Benton for her ability to execute my visions over the past two decades, adding her own elegant flourishes and personal touches. We share a passion for skiing, as well as beautiful printed materials.

Patricia Leidy and I met on Facebook. Her talent caught my eye, and her illustrations make me smile. Thank you, Patty, for bringing the ski bunnies to life on the page.

To Lori Spencer Smith—no blood relation, but my soul sister, editor, yogini friend—100,000 thanks.

Thank you to BookMasters, particularly Regina Hamner for her gracious assistance with this project.

# FRIDAY JONES PUBLISHING AND THE ARTS & CRAFTS MOVEMENT

## FRIDAY JONES PUBLISHING

*Laid-Back Skier's* cover and page layouts, and Friday Jones Publishing's logo and philosophy draw inspiration from the Arts & Crafts Movement, in particular William Morris and Kelmscott Press, and also the Roycrofters. A movement that valued the beauty of nature, the importance of books, hands-on craft, joy in work, and women's creative contributions, the Arts & Crafts influence also is reflected in the fonts, dingbats, and other graphic elements found in *Laid-Back Skier.*

Cover and page design by Colleen Smith and Nancy Benton.
Illustrations: Patricia Leidy
Angel bookplate: *William Morris Designs*, Dover Publications Inc.
Hand-rendered snowflakes by Nancy Benton.
This book features Willow, Garamond and Copperplate fonts.
A Zaph Dingbat snowflake adorns page numbers.
*Bentley's Snowflakes*, W.A. Bentley, Copyright 2006 by Dover Publications, Inc.
Printed on: 100# birch Mohawk Loop Antique Vellum, an environmentally responsible paper.

*Coming 2011*
## ONLY WILD PLUMS

by Colleen Smith

*Only Wild Plums* introduces readers to the Larkins, a large, quirky, Irish-Catholic family living in Colorado. Narrated from the points of view of seven well-drawn characters, the novel details intimate and memorable portraits of a mother, five of her children, and one of her grandchildren—each walking through one of life's major turnstiles. Rich with detailed description; complex relationships; and witty, true-to-life dialogue, *Only Wild Plums* examines clannish bonds and the truth that sometimes family has nothing to do with blood.

FridayJonesPublishing.com  ❈  Join us at Friday Jones Publishing on Facebook.com
Follow FridayPublisher on Twitter.com

FRIDAY JONES
∷ PUBLISHING ∷
WAG YOUR TAIL™